READING SVEVA

ALSO BY DAPHNE MARLATT

Ana Historic

At the River's Mouth: Writing Migrations

Between Brush Strokes (with Frances Hunter)

Ghost Works

The Given

The Gull

How Hug a Stone

Net Work: Selected Writing (edited by Fred Wah) *

Our Lives

Readings from the Labyrinth

Salvage

Steveston (with Robert Minden)

Taken

This Tremor Love Is *

Touch to My Tongue

Two Women in a Birth (with Betsy Warland)

Zócalo

Liquidities: Vancouver Poems Then and Now *

* Available from Talonbooks

READING SVEVA
DAPHNE MARLATT

TALONBOOKS

Talonbooks
278 East First Avenue, Vancouver, British Columbia, Canada V5T 1A6
www.talonbooks.com

First printing: 2016

Typeset in Garamond
Printed and bound in Canada on 100% post-consumer recycled paper

Interior and cover design by Typesmith

Cover reproduced from centre panel of triptych *Foundation I: Passage Over a Foundering Landscape* (1983), by Sveva Caetani, used with permission from the Alberta Foundation for the Arts.

Talonbooks gratefully acknowledges the financial support of the Canada Council for the Arts, the Government of Canada through the Canada Book Fund, and the Province of British Columbia through the British Columbia Arts Council and the Book Publishing Tax Credit.

LIBRARY AND ARCHIVES CANADA CATALOGUING IN PUBLICATION

Marlatt, Daphne, 1942–, author
      Reading Sveva / Daphne Marlatt.

Poems.
ISBN 978-1-77201-016-9 (PAPERBACK)

      1. Caetani, Sveva, 1917–1994 – Poetry. I. Title.

PS8576.A74R43 2016   C811'.54   C2016-904640-0

CONTENTS

Introduction to a Gifted Life 1

I Between Brush Strokes 11

II Reading Sveva 33

    the hand promised 41

    miraggio 45

    a mesh of force 46

    a version 49

    harbouring 50

    Beo 52

    just asking 53

    impelling forces 54

    sidewalk and tower 55

    Petra in Vernon 56

    death. dearth. death 57

    the ongoing 58

    calling 59

    generational 60

    Billy's Hill 61

    gifts 63

    nook a nok 64

    snapshots 65

    the subject 66

    for now 67

    angels of poetry 68

    beast litany 69

    Workmanship 70

    driving at 71

Sources 73

Image Credits 75

Acknowledgements 77

A stage which is lit by anything as tremendous as a near-by star, and whose dark is an endless wheel of enigmatic lights can never be "mundane."

— SVEVA CAETANI

INTRODUCTION TO A GIFTED LIFE

Reading Sveva began with two gifts, one given and one received. The first gift was an appointment I booked with a massage therapist for my partner, Bridget, in 2006. While waiting for her at the clinic, I picked up an Okanagan tourist magazine, mostly about vineyards and wineries, but tucked away on a back page was a brief column with a photograph of the Vernon painter Sveva Caetani, one of her vivid paintings, and a brief sketch of her life. In those few column inches, I met a woman artist who was forced to live in isolation with her widowed mother for twenty-five years, and who, for much of that time, was forbidden from doing what she loved most: painting. And yet, she emerged into her own remarkable vision and art. How she must have struggled for belief in herself and her talent. Sveva died in 1994 at the age of seventy-six. I had to find out more about her.

The second gift came from a simple question I subsequently asked writer and art collector Brian Dedora, who had grown up in Vernon: Do you remember an Italian Canadian artist named Sveva Caetani? He certainly did and one of his memories is embedded in the first paragraph of "snapshots" in the "Reading Sveva" section of this book. Brian dropped into MacLeod's Books where he found and gave me a copy of Heidi Thompson's collaboration with Sveva, *Recapitulation: A Journey*, published by Heidi in 1995, a year after Sveva's death.

Recapitulation contains marvellous full-colour photographic reproductions of the complete series of fifty-six symbolic paintings about her life and her time, along with Sveva's commentaries on each painting, as well as poems in the three languages she spoke (French, English, and Italian). It introduced me to her vibrant painting and in equal measure, to her joyous embrace of life and her antipathy towards the meanest and most violent aspects of the human psyche. Here was an artist who had lived most of her life in small-town Vernon but whose intellect found deep sources in Christian, European, Muslim, Jewish, Hindu, and Buddhist cultures, as well as Western philosophy and contemporary scientific research into the atom and the universe. A child immigrant, the only daughter of an Italian aristocrat who was also an internationally recognized scholar of Islam, Sveva had lived a privileged and highly cultured life until his death when she was in her teens, after which she was forced to live in seclusion and mourning with her widowed mother. At the age of forty-three, suddenly liberated by the death of her mother, a death she also grieved, she came out into the world of Vernon and had to earn her own living for the first time. Remarkably, none of this deterred her "great gusto for Art and Life."[1]

And so began my curiosity about Sveva Caetani and my admiration for her as an intellectual seeker and visionary narrator of her own life with its immense transitions. This curiosity led me to take several trips to the Vernon Museum and Archives to pore through Sveva's papers that were available to the public, and to eventually view half a dozen of her *Recapitulation* paintings at the Alberta Foundation for the Arts. My first response to Caetani's life and work was a long poem published in 2008 as a JackPine Press chapbook, *Between Brush Strokes*, included here in its entirety with a few revisions.

The generosity of gifts – the gifts we inherit and the gifts we are subsequently given – prompts us to offer further gifts to others. This generosity colours the whole of Caetani's life and work, a colour I hope these poems in turn manage to offer.

FROM ROME TO VERNON

Sveva Caetani's life began in Rome where she was born in 1917, a birth that left her mother, Ofelia, ill for several years. Ofelia Fabiani, daughter of a wealthy engineering family in Rome, was the delicately beautiful love of Leone Caetani, son of a centuries-old aristocratic Italian family and an equally aristocratic English mother. As the eldest son, Leone had inherited the family titles of Duke of Sermoneta, Prince of Teano, and was married to Vittoria Colonna, daughter of a family that had feuded with the Caetanis for generations. This intellectually extraordinary man who spoke eleven languages was also a world traveller, an internationally recognized scholar of Islamic history, principal author of the groundbreaking ten-volume *Annali dell'Islam*, Member of the Italian Chamber of Deputies, and a strong socialist. His marriage was an unhappy one and, soon after performing a year of military service during World War I, he met and fell in love with Ofelia Fabiani with whom he had a daughter, Sveva. Disturbed by the rising current of fascism in Italy, he relinquished his titles to his brother and, in 1921, emigrated with Ofelia and Sveva to small-town Vernon where he bought some acres in the BX[2] area and became a gentleman orchardist and self-styled logger.

Sveva was three years old when they arrived in Vernon with thirty pieces of luggage, Leone's valet, Ofelia's secretary, and an Italian cook.

In 1921, Vernon was a small town of just over three-and-a-half-thousand people, the centre for an active fruit-growing industry in the Okanagan. Leone, who had first encountered British Columbia on an earlier hunting trip to the Kootenays in 1891, had learned that the Canadian government was encouraging "gentleman farmers" to immigrate. Like most such farmers, he probably had no knowledge of the Okanagan or Syilx First Nations whose unceded territory this was, even though by the late 1800s there were two reserves, Long Lake and Priest's Valley, nearby.

Ofelia, habituated to the haute couture salons of Paris, the Roman villa Leone had built for her, Russian novels, and Parisian culture, insisted that each year the family return to Europe for a few months, together with Miss Jüül, her secretary, and what became a series of English governesses for Sveva. They would visit relatives in Rome, London, and southern France, and enjoy their customary stays at distinguished hotels in Monte Carlo, Cannes, or Nice. In Monte Carlo, Sveva delighted in art lessons from the Russian painter, André Petroff. On trips to Paris, Ofelia acquired the latest fashions from Chanel and Vionnet. They dined with friends, went to the opera, watched tennis competitions, visited the Caetani castle in Sermoneta, and stayed with Leone's cousins in England.

Leone and Sveva both became Canadian citizens, Leone motivated politically as well as personally by the ability this would give him to make Sveva his legal daughter. Ofelia, who spoke French and Italian fluently, never became a Canadian and refused to speak English, although she understood it. Leone, together with his manager, Guido Manucci, tended fruit trees, felled and hauled logs from his woodlot to the family's large home on Pleasant Valley Road, and sawed and stacked them for their furnace, an actively physical life that gave him pleasure and must have counterbalanced his intellectual pursuits.

He imparted his intellectual curiosity and learning, as well as his pleasure in sustained physical work, to Sveva, who had for company both father and mother, governesses who were often young, as well as the endlessly patient Miss Jüül, and a series of family dogs both large and small with whom she played, but no other children. She displayed a talent for art and was given six months at an art school in Paris.

Marie Jüül, her mother's Danish secretary and companion, had joined the family in Rome while Ofelia was in her long convalescence from Sveva's birth. Dedicated to their well-being, and, as Sveva later remarked, sharing in their joys and grieving with them in their sorrows, she stayed with them and with Sveva for the rest of her life.

A DANTEAN JOURNEY BEGINS

The Caetanis' privileged life diminished sharply after the stock market crash of 1929 when Leone's finances were substantially reduced and the European trips and governesses came to an end. In 1930, Sveva, aged thirteen, was sent to Crofton House School in Vancouver, where for the first time she lived in the daily company of other girls and formed friendships. Her second year at Crofton House, however, was suddenly cut short when she developed a serious case of measles, was brought home to recover, and was never sent back. Then, in 1934, Leone was diagnosed with throat cancer and admitted to the Mayo Clinic where he was treated intensively for almost a year. After a brief remission at home, he went to the Vancouver General Hospital where he died on Christmas Day, 1935, a life-changing event for both Sveva and her mother. While at the Mayo Clinic, he sent a telegram to his daughter urging her to memorize the whole of Dante's *Divine Comedy*, perhaps as a way to distract her from worry and grief. It's difficult to know whether he foresaw the subsequent years of his daughter's life. In any case, he willed their Pleasant Valley home in Vernon to her.

After Leone's death, Ofelia, who had a weak heart, went into seclusion for twenty-five years, taking Sveva with her. Ties to the outside world were cut off, although her daughter had not yet completed grade twelve. Sveva was forbidden to leave the property and any letters from her Crofton House friends were intercepted. She was encouraged to read books but painting was forbidden as "a waste of time." Nevertheless she managed to draw a series of cartoons portraying her frustration, each featuring herself as "Beo." Ofelia, always a perfectionist, grew obsessed with dust and so had carpets, curtains, and other hangings removed. In a house pared of comforts, Sveva was required to wash floors daily and minister to a mother who was terrified of losing her. All of this was complicated by reduced means, Ofelia's weakened heart, and the onset of World War II, which placed Ofelia, still an Italian citizen, in a difficult position in Canada.

On New Year's Eve, 1960, Ofelia died, leaving the little money she had to Marie and her Roman property to the Catholic Church. This left Sveva with the necessity of supporting herself and the elderly Marie, always a patient and affectionate second mother to her. When Ofelia died, Sveva was forty-three and had never worked outside her home. She was given a teaching position in the parochial school attached to St. James Catholic Church. On the advice of kindly neighbours, she joined several clubs in Vernon, including the Naturalists' Club, bought a car, and formed a number of lasting and very supportive friendships. She soon realized, however, that she needed to get her teaching certificate and so, with financial help from friends, she moved herself and Marie to

Victoria where she completed her grade twelve, then enrolled for two years at the University of Victoria, gaining her certificate. While there, she took a course from the well-known art educator John Cawood, who encouraged her to take up painting again.

In the summer of 1972, Sveva and Marie returned to Vernon. Hired to teach art and social studies at Charles Bloom Secondary School in Lumby, Sveva rented a little house for the two of them in that small community just east of Vernon. Marie died there the following spring and was buried next to Leone and Ofelia in the family plot in Vernon. Sveva embarked on an intense period of both painting and teaching, soon exhibiting one of her watercolours in a group show of Okanagan artists at the Burnaby Art Gallery. In 1976, she moved back to her Pleasant Valley home and set up a studio for herself while continuing to teach. She had already begun to sketch, in writing, scenes from her life in the form of a spiritual journey based loosely on the structure of Dante's *Divine Comedy*, with Leone as her Virgil figure. In 1978, she began to paint what would become the series of fifty-six images that comprise her vision of contemporary *infernos*, *purgatorios*, and *paradisos*. Tiny figures of Leone, Sveva, and very occasionally Ofelia, poled in a punt-like boat by Leone's cousin Lovatelli as Charon, appear in many of these paintings. From 1975 to 1989, *Recapitulation* preoccupied her. Each painting arose first as an "image-spark" she would draw, then paint in successive layers of dry-brush watercolour and comment on in writing. A rigorous schedule involved painting for several hours in the morning before leaving for Lumby to teach, and then, at the end of each day, painting well into the night. By 1983, with increasing arthritis complicated by diabetes, it was clear she had to retire from teaching and focus her remaining powers on completing her journey. Confined to a wheelchair, holding a brush with difficulty, she made the final paintings of *Recapitulation*.

Throughout the latter part of her life, Sveva's circle of friends, mainly women, continued to support her. She divided her large home into two apartments and in 1985, Joan Heriot, an accomplished landscape watercolourist and close friend, moved in, each woman having her own studio. Sveva's last years were shared with her. Sveva Caetani died in 1994 at the age of seventy-six.

The *Recapitulation* paintings as well as other paintings of hers were shown in a number of regional galleries, largely in solo exhibitions, but also in group ones. In Vancouver, only the Italian Cultural Institute gave her a solo show, this in 1991. Two years later her work was given solo shows in Toronto and Ottawa, thanks to the support of the Italian embassy. In 1985 she began donating the paintings from this series in finished groups to the Alberta Foundation for the Arts, where the whole of *Recapitulation* has been archivally framed and stored.

On one level, Sveva Caetani's story can be read as one of delayed immigration; although she had lived for almost forty years in Vernon, until her mother's death she had never participated for any length of time in the Canadian life of the community around her. The children she played with were European cousins whom they visited on their annual trips to London or southern Europe. Although she loved being up in the BX orchard and woods with her father, these were breaks from her routine of studies at home with her governess. In late interviews, she spoke of how Ofelia had brought Rome with her to Vernon, bringing "the Rome of her traditions,"[3] and insisting on its maintenance. Leone's English was polished, he had grown up speaking it in his family, but although Ofelia knew the language she refused to speak it, preferring French. Only after Ofelia's death could Sveva enter the life of the town she had lived in for so many years.

In her remarkably generous written portrait of her mother in *Recapitulation,* Sveva describes Ofelia as "a star, whose furnace and pulses net surrounding space in a mesh of force, binding on its partners, or even the passer-by." She acknowledges how this power can be "self-destroying" but extends its otherworldly resonance when she asserts that her mother was "a seeress, absorbed in being the guardian of mysterious gifts [...] magical in her capacities of steely will and divination."[4] When Ofelia was dying, Sveva asked, "Mother, what is going to happen to me?"[5] Ofelia, whose interception of letters from her daughter's friends had left Sveva feeling there was no world for her outside the prison of their home, replied: "you are going to have good friends."[6]

Although as a child she wrote and drew adoring birthday cards for her mother, or "Mau," Sveva readily admits her deep affection was for her father, who encouraged her to excel at whatever she did. While she was still at Crofton House, he advised her: "All other things that we enjoy in life (love included!) turn to bitterness, but a great work and devotion to art are joys that never leave or betray you."[7] Early in her work on *Recapitulation,* when she had already become a successful teacher and artist while aging into "loosened flesh, grey matter, cramped bones,"[8] she wrote a several-page long poem in which she imagines meeting her father again, asserting a deep kinship with him in these lines:

> *For this tall Virgil*
> *In accepting this new stranger in myself,*
> *There may be a restating of concordant minds, parallel spirits,*
> *Tangent souls that can legitimately confront*
> *Each other's otherness.*

What particularly interests me in *Recapitulation* is the way her work couples autobiographical content with social commentary in dry-brush watercolour paintings that glow with a visionary intensity. Karen Avery, in her thesis on the autobiographical narrative of these serial paintings, notes how Sveva represents herself as "a moving character in a drama" so that "the subjectivity in *Recapitulation* is in a constant state of flux."[9] This could not be otherwise for an artist interested in paradox, in movement (as a driver she was a chronic speeder), in energy and its materialization in the universe.

Although I was intrigued by the complexities of the Caetani family romance, what increasingly drew me to Sveva's work is the ontological question expressed in much of her writing: What is the role of human consciousness in the larger orders of the cosmos?

Sveva was a thinker, and for her, painting was mediated by language. She must have welcomed Cawood's theory that "creative activity is the result of mental innovation rather than visual imitation."[10] She seems to have initially conceived her project as a poetic one. Her poems, like diary jottings, are constructed of statements and questions, sometimes rhetorical, often sincere. A sense of dramatic address informs their style. Through them, and through her prose commentaries on the paintings, she probes her European heritage and her relationships with both mother and father, citing sources as diverse as Dante, Rilke, Giacomo Leopardi, Gershom Scholem, Milton, Islamic tradition, W.H. Auden, and Annie Dillard. Socially astute in critique, her poems record the thoughts of a passionate mind examining life experience within the larger spheres of Italian culture, Canadian contemporary life, and the multicultural traditions of the human spirit.

As she moves through the Catholic structure she takes from Dante, from the brutality of man-made hells to the angels of inspiration, Sveva's prose fragments develop a contemporary environmental consciousness – "Our earth is not an ark floating on until fresh living space emerges, but an inescapable planet being devoured of air, space, and purity."[11] The work, both visual and written, transmits wonder at Earth's phenomenally various display of species: "Every detail is honed and developed to the nth degree – fantastic variety, efflorescence, colour, shape, co-ordination and scope,"[12] which she portrays in a major painting titled *Workmanship*, the last to be painted in the series. Against this she sets the small-mindedness and fear that drives much human behaviour. Catholic at root, she reaches toward a large vision when she describes God as "the Great Wave – at times thundering onshore to our small continent of stars, at times heaving far out in the ocean of the cosmos, towering unseen to His own giant rhythms."[13]

Time preoccupies Sveva as her brief years of active life draw to a close. In a long unpublished essay of several drafts, titled "Exploration," she examines concepts of time, language, event, and what we understand as reality, examining how our subjectivity both limits and informs each of these. She is aware of the mediation of language in experience and knowledge. In 1990 she wrote an open letter to Stephen Hawking in response to *A Brief History of Time* in which she complains of the limitations of "a causally structured language" and goes on to say "No syntax (that I know of) possesses a tense or formula that expresses futurity not as a state *following* 'now,' but as it actually is, viz:- the emerging edge of event itself."[14] She refers to time and causality as "our own contrivances for self-location within event while existing on the edge between two worlds, or rather between one void and one reservoir of unrealized possibilities."[15]

Self-awareness meant for her an understanding of how we are all apprehending particles in waves of inter-relation, mind-bodies embedded in what we know of history, culture, our immediate surroundings, pervaded by the unknowable energies of the cosmos. She would concur, I think, with Marilynne Robinson's definition of this kind of awareness as an active engagement of "the self that stands apart from itself, that questions, reconsiders, appraises."[16] It is this questioning mind that is so apparent in much of her writing.

For several years now, I have lived with Sveva's thought embodied in the paintings of her *Recapitulation* series and in her writing. Although I knew nothing about her while she was alive, her letters and recorded interviews in the Caetani archive in Vernon convey a strong sense of the person she was. My poems address her frequently as "you," a mark of how much my thinking about her work and life became an intimate engagement. In these one-sided dialogues with her, I have tried to read some of the energy of her questioning, reconsidering, and appraising "self."

NOTES

1   From the Vernon School District's tribute to Sveva Caetani on her retirement from teaching in 1983, quoted in *Caetani di Sermoneta: An Italian Family in Vernon, 1921–1994*, ed. Catherine Harding (Vernon: Vernon Museum and Archives, 2003,) 27–28.

2   BX: a rural area north of Vernon at that time, named after the BX Ranch, a large acreage and stables for horses of the nineteenth-century Barnard's Express, later BC Express Stage Line, which delivered mail and goods as far north as Barkerville.

3   Interview with CBC's Vicki Gabereau, 1991, Caetani fonds, Vernon Museum and Archives, Vernon, BC.

4   Sveva Caetani, *Recapitulation: A Journey*, eds. Heidi Thompson, Angela Gibbs Peart, Dennis Butler (Vernon: Coldstream Books, 1995), 87.

5   Gabereau interview, 1991.

6   Ibid.

7   Letter from Leone Caetani to Sveva Caetani, 1931, quoted in "The Caetani Family: Popes, Princes, Scholars and Artists," by Karen Avery in *Caetani di Sermoneta: An Italian Family in Vernon, 1921–1994*), ed. Catherine Harding (Vernon: Vernon Museum and Archives, 2003), 13.

8   Typescript of "Echoes for a Reunion" by Sveva Caetani, 1978, Caetani fonds, Vernon Museum and Archives, Vernon, BC.

9   Karen Avery, "The Elusive Self: Storytelling and the Journey to Identity in Sveva Caetani's Autobiographical Series, *Recapitulation*" (MA thesis, University of Victoria, 2003),12.

10 Cawood quoted in *From Drawing to Visual Culture: A History of Art Education in Canada*, ed. Harold Pearse (Montreal: McGill-Queen's University Press, 2006), 237.

11 *Recapitulation*, 96.

12 Ibid., 101.

13 Ibid., 114.

14 Manuscript of "Open Letter to Stephen Hawking," by Sveva Caetani, 1990, Caetani fonds, Vernon Museum and Archives, Vernon, BC.

15 Ibid., 8.

16 Marilynne Robinson, *Absence of Mind: The Dispelling of Inwardness from the Modern Myth of the Self* (New Haven: Yale University Press, 2010), 118.

BETWEEN BRUSH STROKES

I breathe with something of your life, and think with something of your mind.

— SVEVA CAETANI

Between Brush Strokes

singing grass – goes still when she tiptoes near –

she squats. hands, probing carefully, part the dry rustle-grasses back on themselves, on dusty sage –

and there it jumps quick sticklike click, grey elbow jut-outs unfold – wings, oh, bright halo afloat on desert air, *farfalla!*

cicada, her father says, that's what people call it here – *non è farfalla, mia figlia* – sikayda. her father knows everything, insects and fruit trees, different languages, desert turning into paradiso.

sì   sì

     che?

   (oh)
         kay da

the lonesome wail of a train sounds somewhere beyond them through the hills of this parched Okanagan land. her father is growing an orchard with his Italian hands, with his bare hands. fresh water and dust, their new leaf, leaves, blossoming. and look, Sveva, there go our secret horses, horses of the imagination, running between the rows. he points them out to her and laughs at her squint in the heat haze.

Re –
how does a painter grow?

she remembers stone walls, archways, bell tower, her father a duke and a prince back in Sermoneta, in Teano. that doesn't matter, he says, because here we are just people among people. true, we have an unbroken line of nobility behind us but, it's up to us to sustain what truly matters in this life –

la linea / Papa Leone / life line
running through the valley bottom
her mother Ofelia traces
the lightest of touch
on her hand

no, no. the soul's journey, he tells her, down its *wonder-river*, through canyons of impasse, through dead citadels, dead seasons of fate,

wonder as integral to him as the pulsing of his blood.

steel line / lead pencil
Caetani leads
and she is following

leaning up against him, feeling the warmth of his arm as he reads out a passage from the book his finger marks for her, smiling up at him, lean nose she loves, steady eyes that hold her in hope as he holds a line from Dante in memory. her Papa, *for whom remote lands and seeming barrenness promised mystery and adventure.* for whom the horses of the imagination roam and run, *rush like rain.*

Recap –

through paint and graphite
child eye trained by a Russian
artist and Paris thanks to
trips back to Europe
Ofelia's compensation for
uprooting from Rome

human, anguished, and inexpressibly lonely

boxcar wail of away, invitation and link to fountains and cathedral bell towers, *la alta moda*, villas of the Caetanis, the Fabianis, *il teatro,* fabulous architecture once their immediate here. now the canyon their train passes through is without habitation – perhaps a lone squatter, an abandoned prospector's shack.

Solo fantasma

the first figure of the dark canyon intaglioed on its wall like a sylph, like an artist's model, leans back on one arm, while the other, darkness between its fingers, rests on clothed knee. black velvet, backless, hugging the contours of a lean body. amid the shadow of dark hair, one ear catches the light. this is the ear that hears presentiment, dark omens presaging the wrong decision. her attitude of rest duplicit: she could leap up in a flash, in grey flesh, fling wide the door to nightmare's anteroom. a child intuits this,

wonders, watching the shadow cross her mother's smile, her sudden no.

"but why, Mama? why?"

"why is not the question, darling Boo."

a mother so fragile in soft clinging skirts, in pearls, in tunic tops – *an aura of snow*, dazzling in black and white photos her father takes – whether demure or strategically posed, and so much smaller than he is. deceptive cover for steel rails of determination. her mother's eyes the eyes of a *seeress*, kohl-lined, haunted by

si bien see sibyl *Sybilla*
syllabic in flashes

haunted and human

the wail of a train
its one-way to

                                        Recap it
                                        grief-carved
                                        canyon a daughter
                                        makes of solitude's
                                        rock walls so late
                                        so long a latent
                                        fountain

tu? who? who is there to play with besides teddies and dolls with their glass eyes? not Miss Jüül, who comes and goes in quick steps through doorways, making travel arrangements, filing correspondence, keeping a practical eye on things. our jewel, her father jokes, our Viking Miss Jüül. our Innkeeper.

who in the long stretches between trips to Europe? not the tutors and governesses with their serious faces. just Doggie and Rachel, Gavroche and especially Cracker, rubbing her face in the fur of his warm tummy he squirms, pretending to bite. what does a dog see?

out of sight of the house, tucking up her skirt, she goes down on all fours with Cracker, seeing lilies from below their lit cups, bushes from the root up, beetles roused from earth burrows in thunder, it must be thunder, of monumental hands, knees, paws. a scuttle on tiny hooves. whatever quickens, runs, hums unnoticed, another world

Solo fantasma

in the dark middle of life's journey, grey sylph's yellow sister, wraithlike within a neighbouring crevice, hungry with shadow sockets for eyes, stares down on that river swirling below. stuck legs merged to rock, one hand on the sandstone overhang that frames her space, warped torso with sad sag breasts, belly big with want, she gazes from the cavern of eternal envy, hidden from

l'esquisse d'un sourire
spirited
      and sketchy
lo schizzo little squirt
sketching her way through
levels and levels

Italian, French, English sound in her intimacies, old sayings, lines of Persian poetry her father quotes. later, from Crofton House, she will write – *Dear Daddy and Mother, I'm terribly thrilled to learn that perhaps I may go out* – to Southlands stables, tea in a Granville Street café, boarding school English. so the Depression that limits her father's assets, curtailing tutors and trips to Europe, pushes her out into the giddy sociability of school in Vancouver, her friends' banter, their poses overlaid on her father's reflectiveness, her mother's intuition which she misses. *I am always talking about you two very proudly.* On her desk their likeness sits in a framed display, eliciting comments: they *ask me whether the lady is my sister or my self and the man a er – boy friend or a gentleman friend!!!*

she traces the hint of a smile, half-following ups and downs of mood while shading in the contours of a friend's confiding face, soft line of cheek as she listens, catching images of how to be a Canadian girl. and underneath this time, striated lines of rock she cannot see,

Solo fantasma

looming from canyon wall, another sister caverned under blue and yellow fractures in the cliff face. mud dark, head bent, turquoise-lined shoulders, hands arrested on one knee. lost in her own fixity, she bears the heaviness of fate on those strangely lit shoulders.

somewhere, far off and barely heard in the city, the wail of a train.

Ofelia writes that she is no longer to accompany the other girls to Anglican Church on Sundays. "you are to attend Mass, as you should, and as I have advised the headmistress."

> "but why, Mother? why?"
> "you, a good Italian daughter…"

> > mais c'est
> > *Cher Dieu* still –
> > no?

> > *Pouvoir indivisible*
> > sì o no?

> > > a sudden break a
> > > swerve

Recapitu –
the one real tu
disparu

can yon
can He

cancel

cancer

oh no, o prier
please

despite all such words, her father, scholar and just man, lover of Dante, voyageur, steps
out of his *wonder-river* long before wife or daughter are ready. Sveva sits alone in
the empty rooms of their house, stunned in the absence of the bond between them.
moving back and forth, their "angel" Miss Jüül brings appetizing dishes to Ofelia who
waves them away. ushers in the local Padre with his ritual words of consolation. brings
messages to Sveva, "your mother says that any book you need you will find in your
father's library." memorize the *Divine Comedy* he advised.

but no drawing paper, no paints. "a waste of time," Ofelia rules. "if you love me
you will not."

                    "but why, Mother? why?"

nul, nothing but floors to be scrubbed, rescrubbed. perfect grief is clean and keeps
to itself you see

che? che cosi? what?

Rome from the gatepost in
her keeping perfect

in the dark a train, its lonesome wail echoing through some canyon where the vermillion
figure of blue lightning, *enchained Sybil,* visionary flash on the underside of a woman's
persona, stares blindly from cliff face. frozen genie, emanation of stone, she overlooks
the river running at the foot of their canyon elsewhere.

Recapi

tu

lat(e

i( )n

the comfort of her father's study, dust-free and so empty without the dark shock of
his head bent over blueprint or page, her hand lingers on a volume she knows. *Nel
mezzo del cammin di nostra vita / mi ritrovai per una selva oscura . . .* she hears his voice,
its familiar tones inhabiting the words, their rise and fall . . . *là dove terminava quella
valle / che m'avea di paura il cor compunto . . .* sitting down, she begins at the beginning, a
journey she hadn't imagined for herself. she will follow his voice with her stricken heart,
see where her father's horses might lead . . .

You can never know . . .

The image comes to me first . . .
and without warning.

years later, she will paint her mother young, in an Italianate harbour of dream
surrounded by prowling sphinxes, Ofelia in windblown white dress and cape, Ofelia
under stylish black hat, choosing to remain onshore with her riddles despite her
daughter's hand imploring her to join them, she and her father, her father's cousin,
poling their way through blue currents down this *wonder-river* of ever-running time –

"why not, Mother? why not?"

winged sphinxes not flying but crawling. riddle of stubborn determinates? so the
woman seer blind-sided, folds her wings and shrinks, *self-caught.* pity? love? what keeps
her daughter bound to a mother so caught?

deprived of friends, nowhere to go (a train, its haunting whistle of the impossible now
that implausible war rages across Europe, bombs and soldiers in every villa. *The Djinns
for our Dismemberment,*)

in private hell, reading, re-reading a way out

of that phantasmic canyon where, hooded, the colour of dried blood with empty-socket
eyes, chin resting on one hand, sister of desolation, sister of no-can-do, stares into
nightmare above the river where, balanced in the prow of their boat, a minute Leone
will pull the ghost of Ofelia, pull her footless from the wall in his daughter's dream of
redemption,

retrieved, *re*

capitulation

for twenty-five years, for as long as her mother continues, heart-sick, to live, Sveva keeps
house, keeps to house and garden, reads her way through her father's books, walks the
dogs around the garden, occasionally breaches the gate with Miss Jüül on a quick foray
to Vernon bank or post office,

doesn't touch a paint tube, a single brush. imprisoned storm, unwept cataract.
learning how to navigate internal weather by word alone

a line of words   a line of tiny beetles

dot dot   che che? what feet

lead her pencil leading
into not-word, beyond

Ofelia gone.

L'addio è mio.

and she wept, having lost the battle to save her mother in her mother.

after the afterwards, she will look out the window, thinking what? cosi luminoso? –
heat-stilled, dog-sprawled, over-exposed. on her own two feet she will go out – light
falls like an axe –

walk to the gate where their trees have grown tall greens and blues. in a rustle of trans-
parent door opening, air, immense architecture of memory, the green of pine and gold of
artemisia and sage she is *the extension and abbreviation of* sve si sveglia sveva

          si si o glory
                    o colore

that lintel of light where time will be

rivering through brush-stroke and seeing
nameless.

A Deep Transparency (1985)

Villa Miraggio (1981)

Her (1980)

Harbour with Sphinxes (1982)

To Ganesha: The Good Companions (1987)

Workmanship (1989)

READING SVEVA

I feel precipitate. I have come to the hurrying of time.

— SVEVA CAETANI

Portrait of Sveva by Heidi Thompson (1982)

Ofelia, Leone, and Sveva Caetani on the front lawn of their home in Vernon (1927)

Studio portrait of Ofelia in white mantilla (c. 1929)

Sveva Caetani, age thirteen, painting in the south BX, overlooking Vernon and Okanagan Lake (1930)

the hand promised

Child,
birth-pledged to dreams,

        inherent through bloodline dream coheres myriad Akbar's Fatehpur Sikri
abandoned Caetani villa on Gianicolo highest of hills oh Roman claxon soar Miraggio
multi-perspective view a fade-out under jags of dream graph more like flame eating
up egress via fascist singular correctness vision decries

        handprint plain in dew
white-socked on stonecrop fragrant ground it's new your sagebrush pup run clear
as dawn's earliest unbuilt hills

        ghost of a hand (dealt) a future
colours dawning spark

        always to be on the threshold, the foot promised /
its advance, or the hand

        from adorable Beo from Beo's small hand-drawn gifts
to Mou who longed for *il bel mondo* not for Beo of sketchy growth self-caricature
long-shanked knob-kneed reader intent with specs and Islamic taqiyah would-be
architect reading her way alone through stacks of thought

were his, as you were his,
papa morte, guide

gave you his name
in the eyes of the state
non-Italian
        world-embracing
intellect of rational investigation
Annali dell'Islam

turned gentleman orchardist
woodcutter democrat
Canadian

The man my mother and I knew was
gentle, humorous, observant and

that word for active intelligence
enchanting.

*   *   *

then what was handed to you?

Flood-veined
the woman
Imprisoned storm

           climbing walls
           three bleeds the same
           in Catholic purdah

         walls become floors
         scrubbed daily

under constant erasure

       close-up : Sveva
       daughter devoted
       and friendless for
       twenty-five years

     per amor di _____! (unclear)

non è permesso

         sketch hand stilled
techne immured in the unsure inadequate *re*
faith

(in ?

maternal strictures structure
material fear

accept

cleanliness is next to _____

lifeline unclear

* * *

Freed to feel
The trackless pull and push

to walk out with plus de rien there's the house still Marie who supports / to
support hand-stitched altar cloth prize-winning rug design break out a whirl of
Mackie House Paddy *happy Sunday Scrabbly* Joan Naturalist Club Twink parties
gossip letters the means never enough to coast for teacher training stimulus return
dry-brush technique those young faces fire *my children* means awake at five to paint
Cain, Zeus mourning inner dark light teach en courage the leap across

for this great up-welling,

the choice here has been

what is lived
from event to
invent

* * *

a knowing hand, your *fading eye*

combat that empty space
line alone commands
a spell or spells it out

Severance where

the bursting heart
Must stop

        still   heart in the work never stops a passionate dance for eyes or ears   that equivocal comma doubling sense / mind in the work of *para* before *doxa*   only eye and hand keep self from stoppage   an eye away from hand long gone will see   no stop *miraggio*

palazzo dream transfer dry grass *miracolo* this arid this baron's sunlit orchard
mystery how a second-hand hotel turns villa treed with dogs walled Eden world
their own you situate umber earth shadow ochre dry valley lift in darkness up
swept mesa contours their merge or emerge from waterless scape their together
splits you from how archetype leonine hand holds her slim wrist his tender gaze
down her petite face open eyes his dream of adorably fragile *whisper of wings*
a gauzy cover you note her *barriers were for eternity* their greening gone a
prison *like* you wrote but not alike *mirage where their footsteps met* only there
where you buried them in this earth.

a mesh of force

moth(er) wings twilit you mothing a study of *motte* older than butterfly great grey scales you drew sharp-pointed jags clothing her slenderest arms

fifteen entries for moth, eighty-four various mothers, goddess to motherwort

featherlike delicacy

seated on scroll bench mirroring rail (tracks far off) I-beam only I disconnect in so solitary back to the world's eyes gauging that naked nape tender as geisha kimono slips shoulders delicate spine

A rustle of hurt
A whisper of wings

La Parque manqueé

you spiny urchin say,
near smashed her interior
coming out

she, slow-cooled exterior
perfect the *cool blaze of her*

stress concentrated within

closed in her own bologna bottle
Sibyl wings folded in
what you cannot
forgive

disuse

*   *   *

O O O
felia

who took your portrait?

all misty greys except that black clutch of dried leaf/berries attached
to white mantilla wrapped   cold lace   *perfect mouth*   pearl skin madonna
lidded eyes   a luminous   unblinking   gaze

O mirror photo

ritratto in retreat
behind that face

gives nothing
away

*   *   *

immaculateness
that saturated
all her belongings

aura of snow

– in context please, this follows my note about her being a *seeress*.

– you don't say much about her *mysterious gifts* except to say the first of these is beauty.
how did that mark her a *seeress*?

– to live with someone who safeguards her beauty ... well, she couldn't. beauty involves
being seen. after he died there was no one for her, no one who could see her the way he
had.

– so twenty-five years of seclusion then? even for you?

– *Madonna immaculata.* for her there were no greys, only black or white.

self-imposed purdah then
self enclosed in the
myth she was living
amid alien corn
(declined at table)

    grass benches of Vernon's
    lake terrain home /
    sick for Rome

just Pleasant Valley Road

    grief squalls driven
    within four walls

raison d'être for here
politic, principled
gone with him

    in the face of
    economic collapse
    war

"The Lord is near to
the broken-hearted…"

crevecoeur not simply
folded wings but

refus!

this wasn't what she chose
or you, this Okanagan
zenana alone

a version

from outside only
seeing, reading

through dislocation
the local or immediate

self-imposed purdah a phase
night of lunar eclipse

various darknesses require

dream theatre lights architectural
memory embodies the grand
histrionic elsewhere

was she your dark guide through grief?

love so called

upon, potent in
limitations

harbouring

your 1921 harbour
weight of historic culture
looking back, *castello* crowned

the dearly known

slight figure surrounded
by catlike sphinxes
quayside she waits
hesitates svelte
twenties white dress
windblown

from offshore it comes
change blowing sphinx
wingscarves and waves

"*Nothing stays,*" so Lovatelli /
Charon

poles his skiff through
to reach you and your light-
rimmed, left
wing father guide
ready to forgo
palazzo and land, il fascismo
organized labour's collapse

      you turning back to
      implore her
      "come"

nel salto, nel voto

small below that towering
age-old face turned to
brutal flank of battle array

she refrains, restrains
her windblown dress, *una donna
del generone* arrayed in
summer white
luminous, intelligent
and yet

self-locating you said
looking back

and yet

each instant we stand on
edge on the
edge of event's
undecidable future

hesitant

Beo

you with the knobby knees, long legs, flat-footed Beo sending missives to Mau,
declaring love, love for lion mother Bast of alabaster skin, inscrutable

e belle, si belle

you outgrowing yourself beside her, you chatty and thin beside mother cat who
held all promise, chatoyant, urbane, mercurial

e feroce

with a cat mother's strength to protect
single-minded

Beo bébé who adored
who would be oh
so much more

than Beo caged mynah or mine. could she have foreseen, so naming you so
young then gangly one cartooning yourself *Beo Bibliotecario, Beo Postino,*
Beo with pen –

you opening yourself to the world?

just asking

root hell its hold
on paradise flower

here in civitas ongoing
sidewalk opt-outs discard
what labels them

your *pietre anonime*

needled

forays in doorways
exit signed

each journey in time's
plastic duration

a hedged bet

a private garden paradise
(in memoriam)

neither Earthly nor
Divine

this city's contested ground
a ware?

the *foundering landscape* of your inheritance nixed by
circumstance, period of looming visages hooded in totalitarian
caldera, Mussolini among them.

to look at beautiful forms even as you cut them,
kaleidoscopic, turn your eye for Italian architecture to
symmetries of reflection, spectrum of tints

architectonic papyri-like flowers you make of Rome's Palazzetto
dello Sport, arches of reinforced concrete shaft into waters
your canoe glides by

(the Vernon hotel Leone made family home, did he know of
pre-settlement kekulis? discuss the struggle for irrigation?)

ornate Roman fountains, water splashing from hills . . .

you recall late Renaissance Il Gesù turned baroque interior,
fourteenth-century Basilica Sancti Petri's "red rock" grave a
foundation from Nero's time, tilted doorways, broken
curves of aqueduct a weight you shear off, identifying this
civilization's im/pediment

foundering
a purgatory of helplessness

running the runes of dicta you said
we take for the real

sidewalk and tower

hand dangle helpless
wooden head model blind
string jointed, missing

he's King Mannikin you set
in *burrows of nightmare*
oblivious to them below

even the monkey at their back
can read their names

illegal, migrant, homeless
parasite casualties
of their *sfortuna*

      embodied, a crowd
      on grey cement

he sprawls above
replica wooden man-no-kin
at ease on green for profit
in the bag he thinks
success justifiably his
and no relation to

a world at large
gone missing

Petra in Vernon

haunted by water this valley dry of creeks, Swan once Nintle Moos Chin
"jumping over place where the creek narrows" settler Girard built his log
cabin by BX now trickles under a paved road behind motel pool gas exhaust
a shimmer really weedy trees how widow weeds back then might ghost
Ophelia's drowned face a spectral hairfan going nowhere or Shalott's
locked lady high in a room dreaming the world by river reflected in
that mirror books supplied and plied you with images of another real
beyond Patou's consoling shepherd-pacing mother's limits you at eighteen
in forced seclusion blocked a longing deep in *stores of deprivation* burst
eventual flow a rush you paint in Petra's pour from hidden cistern rock cleft
ancient passion streams *slip-loosed* a vision world she stands watch against
apart alone denying self or comfort you so young *so passion comes* at last
wild from stony lack of change the liquid glow your later years perform.

death. dearth. death

here or on the way
there where options shrink
in the dark ink
of night's Mediterranean

who dared call it
Mare Nostrum?

who was speaking plural
possession behind each
border guard?

war you called
a game of barter

human community cut up

brutal chance operations
economic engines failing
the progress narrative

the wavering
signature of community
torn up

the ongoing

from the bottomless immeasurable (without complexity) of Dantean
hell you picture Cruelty's moloch mouth fanged empty-
eyed and wide-spread finger grope for youth below

while Envy looms in bony reptile skin, hissing

1979

IRANIAN REVOLUTION, CHINESE INVASION OF VIET NAM, CIVIL WAR IN
EL SALVADOR, IRA KILLINGS, SEIZURE OF MECCA'S MASJID AL-HARAM...

behind the everyday features of mankind

by 1984 old jags rise icy under transparent razor path

AMRITSAR'S GOLDEN TEMPLE INVASION, GANDHI ASSASSINATED, MASS
KILLING OF SIKHS, IRA BRIGHTON BOMBING, ETHIOPIA'S FAMINE...

suspended over an abyss your skeletal artery-netted feet step-step a razor blade
(you without use of your legs or not without pain by then) not the pre-supposed
but poised *To place a second ... after the agony and terror of the first ...* without
goal, reiteration each the only

step
    along
            the blade that cuts

                        connecting...

calling

called artist
called "our countess"
called a character

context small-town Vernon
between lakes

context Rome, London
Teano, Paris

a calling for colour, line
commit to

sudden astonishment

called to definition
transient recognition

lingual world in flux

call it struggle
with Eden's
law from without

call it *la joie, gioia*
never left

you, ardent for

horizon line, a shared
perceptual event

generational

imprint the Passion no imprimatur to recapitulate generations of belief where cutting words or lines incise grief's arid valley gated Eden's closed for sixteen years then plumber electrician necessary intervenor all's grist for still Christos suffering ergo *if, if you loved me you would not* ... familiar interdict this who do you think you are? of gender weight mother edict capital despite deep sift for interspeak to plumb uprush embrace of what's unseen outside.

Billy's Hill

Now his people call it
by his name

turn-off door
empty chill echoes
reluctant fear, small
hands strapped raw
failure to understand
this foreign, this
brutal

who says? say what?
not in your language

residential school grab
Syilx children
in exile

. . .

on hands and knees cleaning
cleaning begins again the same
floored by/to
exacting standards

(in reverse

. . .

wipe-out of what
can't be understood,
controlled

(this Earth now

...

you understood Billy's gunning it, his
clench grin mad uphill drive to
make his mark

in the face of
mass wipe-out:

wordless

gifts

given linguistic
ebullience

given Italian, French, English
some Hebrew, a little
Arabic

given inner restraint

given laughter, light

given vision's far reach
and care, curious
unorthodox

what it means
this unique, this

intimate link

here in

not after

nook a nok

so drawn to reading you enclosed comfort medieval close or closet wood wall
(crucifix there) under arcade nook defence from breezeway foot traffic ignores
scrutiny yours of words but more beloved you draw in/under cloister arches warm
handprint pages note your stand-in for Jane Austen quill raised thought burst hurt
sequence sparks your *keyboard* of internalized generations' worth a series of steps
Dante in red scholar gown descends hand extended White Guelf gone with centuries
politics now literary lineage invoked you honour your ghostly father out of time's
corner mind's syntax of loves this cubbyhole historic sweep arcade flesh holds
reading imprint a trace a nok books conjure learning marks not marketing this
solitary reader.

snapshots

walking down Main Street on your way to the bank, one of your few permitted outings, you know Ofelia is counting the minutes. a gaggle of fifties kids watch you walk tall, poised in thirties slacks, cloche hat, outdated style, Miss Jüül small beside you. they think she's a karate expert, there to protect you from teenage loungers, wolf whistles, catcalls.

– a mother so terrified of losing control

on the eve of the sixties, caring for that same mother, bedridden now, your world reduced to the prison of her room, you grieve as she dies slowly, immobilized by her still-Roman heart,

– she longed not for pomp and circumstance – but for what was pared and polished and worked to perfection

in the smell of chalk and sweat you talk the history of thought to high-school students, passionata, you walk them through art, life, *the journey of the soul,* their bodies thrum to the Stones, gender pulse, speed, communal rush at the pubs

to give what your father gave: *unparalleled initiation … into the world of the mind*

via easel and paint, shadow of plum across a remembered wall, flush of birds outside visit your mind as psalm, *laud* in the soar of image, live sparks you bring out of words into saturate colour, coming home to the open

potential event-possibility – on the edge of chaos,

in your living room, regal in wheelchair, arthritic legs no longer letting you *stand on my own two feet*, you offer this house you leave in legacy, history, names of builders, kind-hearted neighbours, your first car, even the taxi driver your Pyrenees dogs would allow to your then-closed door,

Caetani history bleeds into the story of Vernon, you and your parents muralled above parked cars.

the subject

you can never know

or abject? shadow woman, she stands alone, barefoot, listening, right hand
clasping her other wrist – those long legs, long arms, they're yours, head down,
waiting for? the vibration you call God *in a universe of vibration and wave*

in the pain of arthritic wrist, hand that won't hold a brush to precision strokes,
clasping a wrist, arrest

in wave upon wave of descending letters

the subject you have given up, in this the third-to-last you paint, not language
in its receding tideline need to make sense of this complex transiency life is,
ONLY LOVE, large across knobby knees

the human self-image ... not even valid as a discard

voices surround you, children, those you taught to see what seeing can create,
varicoloured worlds you're beginning to leave but hearing hear the prompt
through *portages of pain, / Headwaters of lostness,* a wave that lifts, shakes
limbs in audible caress, wind-rush you love, the THIS coming in, in,
to subside into empty air again.

for now

taking that step across, into

landscapes of which we are both the extension and the abbreviation,

particulars grown luminous

only breath and an opening

your angels muscular and masculine
waver outlines of flow
time's boat navigates through
light pour, pulse

degrees of reprise Rilke's
Israfel strums you

listen walk ponder Orfeo's glance
memorial to muse a nacht musique
surprised, on the verge of sleep

breaks up through vents in the prescribed
all winds and broken chords, limbs in
sinuous, a part writing

beast litany

as if on a last soon-to-be lost *Ararat*, this mountain of beasts, *Congress of Kings*, elephant by springbok, muskox by anaconda, grey whale in a splash from rising seas. these *good companions* you depict, each at peak strength, equal in presence with Ganesha, whose ears flare to hear their cries,

Destroyer of Evils and Obstacles, dancing Deva, golden trunk you paint in a curl holding what tray of sweets? in hand, elephant goad, not for the animal who supports him, broad back instead of the usual mouse (sneak thief, harvest robber), but gentle and large like himself, trunk not lopped (nor head, for that matter, market ivory)

god with a goad, an "a"

this wildlife Ark on a roiling ground of red (wildfire of our own making?), tiny canoe across an upper corner, and there in it, mother and father, both. turning to face them you point to that mountain of beings – wild and not so free – toward Ganesha,

ironic deity / Atop self-indulgent human meat – ah, those sweets simply sugar-loaded enticements then for this

prose human body … spendthrift of living / Wanton with death. both goad and sweets for us, our appetites that consume our kin, yet you declare *the worst intrusion / Eden – without man*

reserving potential for *reverence halfway deeper / Than lament,*

by halves then, would-be gods, half reverent, half seeing what we consume.

Workmanship

arthritic bone knobs
boutonnière deformity dip
ochre and ivory wrinkled
fingers of one hand warming
stiffness of the other

another you state with a capital
Creator, these so human hands
between brush strokes

you depict central to
this your final your
intricate fractal-based
aquatic and terrestrial
cornucopia sleeves

creative excess of Earth
your fingers presage leaving

… field of that cosmic attraction concentrated inwardly

furred moth crayfish coral and geranium petal scaled upward from minute
antennae eggs or wing pattern striation fish-eye creature extensions

a fabric as in made
by replication, irrepressible
concentrate of joyous vision
curve and angle, colour

magnified and sheer as in
clear pure water

your co-creation

driving at

where words meet paint

two subjectivities meet
tangential stories seep across
discrete lineages, *this*

keyboard of transmittable memory
language

cognition's shift

fingering alphabet, water colour
dry-brush fusion of hues
results in glow

recognition's ah

if reality is seen as momentum

we speed through
changing perspectives

its drive is to
unceasing erasure as well

that razor line in
finite illusion
infinity's edge

time on your hands
in your eyes on the wheel

never enough

SOURCES

The poems listed below draw from the following paintings in Caetani's *Recapitulation* series and her accompanying poems and commentaries.

Between Brush Strokes
> *Departure from the Canyon of the Dark Sisters* (1984); *A Deep Transparency* (1985)
> and, in passing, *Rendezvous with the Horses of the Imagination* (1884);
> *The Game I: The Djinns for Our Dismemberment* (1985).

a mesh of force
> *Her* (1980), and the photo portrait of Ofelia (1927).

harbouring
> *Harbour with Sphinxes* (1982).

Beo
> Caetani's self-cartoons, particularly *Beo the Librarian* (n.d.).

impelling forces
> *Foundations 1: Passage Over a Foundering Landscape* (1983); *Foundation III: Hoodoos of the Great Caldera* (1984); and *Foundations IV: The Running of the Runes* (1984).

sidewalk and tower
> *King Mannikin* (1979).

Petra in Vernon
> *Petra in the Storm* (1985).

the ongoing
> *From the Abyss: The Razor's Path* (1984).

Billy's Hill
> *Billy's Hill* (1985).

the subject
> *The Voice* (1988).

nook a nok
> *The Nook* (1986).

angels of poetry
> *Presences in the Maelstrom: Angels of Poetry* (1983).

beast litany
> *To Ganesha: The Good Companions* (1987).

Workmanship
> *Workmanship* (1989).

IMAGE CREDITS

Photographs of Caetani's paintings

COVER IMAGE
Centre panel of *Foundation I: Passage Over a Foundering Landscape,* 1983
  Watercolour on paper, 70.2 x 45.5 cm (*Collection of the Alberta Foundation for the Arts 1985.064.018.B. Used by permission of Vernon Public Art Gallery*)

PAGE 25
A Deep Transparency, 1985
  Watercolour on paper, 97 x 59 cm (*Collection of the Alberta Foundation for the Arts 1986.014.002. Used by permission of Vernon Public Art Gallery*)

PAGE 26
Villa Miraggio, 1981
  Watercolour on paper, 89.5 x 75.5 cm (*Collection of the Alberta Foundation for the Arts 1985.064.015. Used by permission of Vernon Public Art Gallery*)

PAGE 27
Her, 1980
  Watercolour on paper, 68 x 51.7 cm (*Collection of the Alberta Foundation for the Arts 1985.064.013. Used by permission of Vernon Public Art Gallery*)

PAGE 28
Harbour with Sphinxes, 1982
  Watercolour on paper, 87 x 59.5 cm (*Collection of the Alberta Foundation for the Arts 1985.064.01. Used by permission of Vernon Public Art Gallery7*)

PAGE 29
To Ganesha: The Good Companions, 1987
  Watercolour on paper, 139 x 80.5 cm (*Collection of the Alberta Foundation for the Arts 1988.017.003. Used by permission of Vernon Public Art Gallery*)

PAGE 30–31
Workmanship, 1989
  Watercolour on paper, 77.5 x 114 cm (*Collection of the Alberta Foundation for the Arts 1989.054.001. Used by permission of Vernon Public Art Gallery*)

Caetani family photographs

PAGE 37
Ofelia, Leone, and Sveva Caetani on the front lawn
of their home in Vernon, 1927
 (*Vernon Museum and Archives 12426*)

PAGE 38
Portrait of Sveva, by Heidi Thompson, 1982
 (*Reproduced with the permission of Heidi Thompson
 and Vernon Museum and Archives 12699*)

PAGE 39
Studio portrait of Ofelia in white mantilla, c. 1929
 (*Vernon Museum and Archives 12728*)

PAGE 40
Sveva Caetani, age thirteen, painting in the south BX,
overlooking Vernon and Okanagan Lake, 1930
 (*Vernon Museum and Archives 12551*)

ACKNOWLEDGEMENTS

Thanks to the Greater Vernon Museum and Archives, the Vernon Public Art Gallery, and the Alberta Foundation for the Arts for granting access to the Caetani archive, and for permission to reproduce the Caetani family photographs. The portrait of Sveva (1982) was taken by Heidi Thompson; my thanks to Heidi for permission to use the photo.

The quotes in the poems come from Sveva's papers in the Greater Vernon Museum and Archive, and from her commentaries and poems in *Recapitulation: A Journey* by Sveva Caetani, edited by Heidi Thompson, Angela Gibbs Peart, and Dennis Butler.

With gratitude to the B.C. Arts Council for two grants that greatly facilitated the writing of this book, the first in 2007 for the writing of *Between Brush Strokes*, and the second in 2014 for time to complete the necessary research and additional writing for this book.

My sincere thanks to the following people who were all instrumental in this book's genesis and production: Barbara Bell at the Greater Vernon Museum and Archives for unfailing assistance on my research trips to GVMA;

Kim Allen, executor, for permission to quote from the Caetani archive, and to Dauna Kennedy of the Vernon Public Art Gallery for permission to reproduce the *Recapitulation* paintings that appear in this book;

Kristin Stoesz and Gail Lint at the Alberta Foundation for the Arts, for kindly arranging for me to see some half dozen of the Caetani *Recapitulation* paintings, pulled from storage and generously discussed with me;

Kevin Williams at Talonbooks for immediate willingness to publish *Reading Sveva*, Ann-Marie Metten for negotiating permission to reproduce the paintings, Shazia Hafiz Ramji for wonderfully close reading and editing, and Les Smith for design;

Heidi Thompson, whose dedication to making Sveva Caetani's work better known was remarkably achieved in the excellent photographs she took of Caetani's paintings that comprise *Recapitulation: A Journey,* as well as in the editing and publishing of that book. For copies of *Recapitulation: A Journey,* write to 9905 Coldstream Creek Road, Vernon BC V1B 1C8;

JackPine Press of Saskatoon for publishing the first section of this book in a slightly earlier version as *Between Brush Strokes* in 2008; many thanks to Frances Hunter for her award-winning design for that beautiful chapbook and thanks to Jill Robinson for introducing me to the press;

Brian Dedora for the copy of *Recapitulation: A Journey* that introduced me to Sveva's art and thought, and for offering me some first-hand memories of Sveva and Miss Jüül;

Sharon Lawrence for organizing my 2011 visit with Joan Heriot to hear memories of her close friendship with Sveva; Susan Brandoli at the Caetani Cultural Centre and Laisha Rosnau for interesting discussions about Sveva and the Caetani family;

Editors Karl Jirgens of *Rampike* (24/1), and Paul Nelson, George Stanley, Barry McKinnon, and Nadine Maestas, editors of the anthology *Make It True: Poetry of Cascadia* (Leaf Press, 2015) who published earlier versions of "the ongoing" and *"a mesh of force"*; rob mclennan who published "Miraggio" in *The Peter Yacht F Club #22* (2015)";

Catriona Strang, Meredith Quartermain, Fred Wah, Pauline Butling, critical readers of this manuscript, with thanks for their insights and responses;

Karen Fleming for my introduction to Sveva Caetani's life and work in that brief article discovered in her waiting room's reading material;

And, as always, my gratitude to Bridget MacKenzie, my life partner, first reader and invaluable research assistant, for her participation in our research journeys and her insight during our many shared conversations about Sveva and her life.

DAPHNE MARLATT was at the centre of the West Coast poetry movement in the 1960s when she studied at the University of British Columbia with several of Donald Allen's New American Poets, notably Robert Creeley and Robert Duncan. Her association with the loosely affiliated TISH group encouraged her non-conformist approach to both form and language.

Her later association and collaboration with Canadian feminist writers led to co-founding and co-editing the bilingual feminist journal, *Tessera*. She also co-founded *periodics* and co-edited *The Capilano Review*, *Island*, and *TISH*.

Marlatt is known for her formally innovative books of poetry, including *Steveston*, *Touch to My Tongue*, *Salvage*, and *Liquidities*. Her novelistic long poem, *The Given*, received the 2009 Dorothy Livesay Poetry Prize. She is also the author of two acclaimed novels, *Ana Historic* and *Taken*, as well as a celebrated contemporary Canadian Noh play, *The Gull*.

In addition to teaching, she has served as writer-in-residence at nine universities across Canada and at the Banff Writing Studio.

In 2006, Marlatt was appointed to the Order of Canada in recognition of a lifetime of distinguished service to Canadian culture. In 2012, she received the George Woodcock Lifetime Achievement Award.

PHOTO: SHAZIA HAFIZ RAMJI